HOPE for the Next Step

HOPE For The Next Step
365 Days of Inspiration and Encouragement

Loretta McNary

HOPE for the Next Step

HOPE for the Next Step: 365 Days of Inspiration and Encouragement

Copyright © 2014 by Loretta McNary

Published/Revised December 2018, by Five Seven Media, Memphis, TN 38119

www.fivesevenmedia.com

All rights reserved. No part of this publication may be reproduced, stored in a retrieval system, or transmitted in any form or by any means—electronic, mechanical, digital, photocopy, recording, or any other—except for brief quotations in printed reviews, without the prior permission of the publisher.

All scripture quotations, unless otherwise indicated are taken from the Holy Bible: King James Version, New International Version, and the New Living Translation.

ISBN 978-0-9841096-4-7

Library of Congress Control Number: 2018913851

Printed in the United States of America

HOPE for the Next Step

HOPE For The Next Step
365 Days of Inspiration and Encouragement

Loretta McNary

HOPE for the Next Step

TO:

_____

FROM:

_____

DATE _____

HOPE for the Next Step

HOPE For The Next Step
365 Days of Inspiration and Encouragement

Loretta McNary

HOPE for the Next Step

Dedication

This book is dedicated back to God. Father, thank You for using me to be a blessing to others. May this book provide the inspiration and encouragement we need on tough days and remind us to make the time to say Thank you every day. I pray "Hope for the Next Step" will be used as a guiding light that always points us straight to You, especially when we feel hopeless and discouraged.

To my darling father, Dave Shorter Jr. (R.I.H. February 17, 1999, and my firstborn son, Brandon Maurice McNary (R.I.H. July 15, 1999). They believed in me way before I believed in myself. I will always cherish them in my heart and soul. And I will forever appreciate their extravagant love and never-ending support of all my business endeavors.

To my mother, my shero, Dorothy Shorter-Peggs, your love and support mean the world to me. To my incredibly awesome sons, Marshall McNary, Nicholas McNary, Spencer McNary and Jacob McNary, thank you all for loving me, being patient with me, and encouraging me to pursue my dreams. To my amazing grandbabies; Kylin Chandler McNary and Naomi Lyric McNary, you fill my heart with so much joy!

HOPE for the Next Step

And to parents who are living with the extreme grasp of grief and pain caused by experiencing the passing of a child; may you always trust God to care for you.

HOPE for the Next Step

Foreword

Loretta Mc Nary, Creator and Television/Radio Show Host, of the "Loretta McNary Show," Founder of the Non-Profits, Pink Eagles/Blue Eagles and Author of "FAITH For The Next Step", is a woman who has answered God's call to encourage and inspire others using the visual and literary media.

"HOPE For The Next Step", is Loretta McNary's second literary work and is a collection of encouraging faith based and insightful passages, quotes and scriptures written to comfort and strengthen those that may at times experience an overwhelming sense of despair. It also provides enlightening introspective advice from a spiritually sound biblical perspective on how to stand in the face of adversity, as well as how to move forward with a sense of boldness and feeling empowered with the ability to strategically take action to bring goals and objectives to fruition.

I truly appreciate the transparency in which this book is written. I was also immensely inspired by Loretta McNary's choice to candidly share numerous nuggets of wisdom, and spiritual truths. Her inclusion of biblical doctrine is a true testament to the genuineness that she has for wanting people of all faiths, nationalities and genders, to be able to

HOPE for the Next Step

journey through each season in their life; confidently knowing that God loves us. And He is always in control of our lives. Our belief in Him gives us the HOPE we need for our next step. Our faith in Him provides everything we need to live our lives with joy, faith and peace.

> Monica R. Emery
> Celebrity Publicist
> MRE & Associates

HOPE for the Next Step

Acknowledgments

To my Heavenly Father whose love, wisdom, favor, mercy, and grace are everlasting, and all I need to live moment-by-moment and day-by-day. I am forever grateful for You choosing me for such a time as this. Without Him, none of what I do would be possible.

To Brandon, whose example of undying love, unyielding support and faith, I am now becoming the woman I was created to become.

To Marshall McNary, whose undeniable desire to be successful in every area of his life, has taught me to set big goals and to never settle for less than the very best in my life.

To Nicholas McNary, whose inexhaustible charm and unrelenting positive outlook for life, encourages me to make time to enjoy life and to look deeper inside my soul for answers.

To Spencer McNary, whose unbending resilience and discipline to be true to his authenticity, dares me to be true to my own uniqueness.

HOPE for the Next Step

To Jacob McNary, whose unparalleled work ethic and unapologetic passion to have the desires of his heart, challenges me to be unstoppable in pursuing my dreams.

To my mother, her silent strength liberates me to seek and find the inner strength I need on those days that seem to challenge me the most.

To my earthly father, who was taken from me way too soon, your robust work ethics and your unique essence of treating everyone with kindness and respect, that you have instilled in me, continues to guide and inspire me daily.

To my wonderful grandchildren, I call them my bonus babies; Kylin Chandler McNary and Naomi Lyric McNary. Kylin and Naomi, you bring me joy on such a ginormous level. Your over-flowing quest to know the answers to life and to push the limits to gain knowledge is so uplifting and contagious. Always know, I love you both completely to infinity and beyond.

To my brother, Larry McNary, my sister, Wanda Parker-Brown, and my sister-in-law, Laura McNary, thanks for loving me.

HOPE for the Next Step

To all my aunts, uncles, cousins, nieces, nephews, grandnieces and grandnephew; I love you all so much and am praying for you all to seek and walk in your individual purpose. To my godmother and my play moms, your love is deeply appreciated.

A hearty and special thank you to all my closest friends for all your prayers, support and friendship; I'm deeply grateful and thankful for each one of you: Mary McNary, Janice Ousley, Juanita Dillard, Kathy Blake, James Robinson, Jr., Tony Johnson, Janice Gatewood, Marilyn Whitney, Bryon Cowan, Terrie S. Reed, Terry Marr, Jan Winterburn, Amelia Cole, Charles and Lori Moscato, Ellen Olford, Sheron Thomas, Glenn Hill, Sr., and so many others.

To my pastors; Rufus Smith, Craig Strickland and Dr. Eli Morris whose Sunday morning messages always help carry me when my own hope wasn't enough for my next step. I continue to learn so much from your servant leadership. To my Hope Church family, thank you for your love.

A BIG thank you to Shelia E. Bell for editing "HOPE for the Next Step" and my first book, "Faith for the Next Step". I appreciate you for believing in my writing ability

HOPE for the Next Step

from the very start. Your multi-NY Times Best-selling author ranking is coming soon.

To my remarkable publicist, Monica R. Emery, thank you very much for your expertise, wisdom, support and encouragement in helping me gain national exposure as a TV Talk Show Host. I appreciate the heart-warming foreword you penned for "HOPE for the Next Step," which you graciously refer to as "my literary work".

HOPE for the Next Step

Introduction

"HOPE for the Next Step" is more than a second book in a trilogy. "HOPE for the Next Step" is a daily dose of inspiration and hope for not only the days and moments that challenge us, but also for the days that are simply good, to remind us to always have a thankful heart. HOPE was initially on target to be published in 2014. However, that is not what happened as you can tell from a publish date of 2018. I could not decide on a title or a cover design.

My goal has always been was to publish this book as a perpetual calendar, so readers could have something to read daily for inspiration, encouragement and to be mentally and spiritually prepared to enjoy a great day. It is written with short, tender, to the point quotes, scriptures, and affirmations to start a day or recharge a moment that has started to shift to the left.

However, after major computer issues, day to day busyness, and a lot of procrastination, "HOPE for the Next Step" was eventually put on the proverbial back burner. This all changed in late October 2018, I was talking to one of my best friends. I mentioned a few of her many achievements and she countered with,

HOPE for the Next Step

but I do not have two books published. I grew quiet for a moment and sadly, said "neither do I." You see, Janice knew I had written a second book and had it professionally edited four years ago. What she didn't know was that I had not decided on a title or a book cover design, and the process was stalled. Why she considered that an accomplishment, I am not sure. Anyway, her comment hijacked my entire thought process for the next few days. I was at a standstill. I felt compelled to finish the book, but how could I? I was planning a major event, working on growing my TV Show nationally, hosting a weekly radio show, along with managing my day-to-day responsibilities.

For three days my spirit was vexed. How can I finish a book with so much going on in my life? Here is the struggle; how could I deny the fact, I was divinely called to write and publish this book so that others would have access to a quick and empowering nugget of HOPE each day. So, I decided to complete what I started in 2014. Once I decided that it was time, I prayed for inspiration for the title and provisions to hire a designer. Two weeks later and a partial re-write, HOPE was ready to be published. God has a very special way of letting us know when "it's time" to move forward. What I thought was

HOPE for the Next Step

procrastination was really extra time to grow as a person and embrace a spirit of transparency; which allowed me to be in full alignment with God's perfect timing. My friend's comment was the push I needed to finish my second book.

I firmly believe had I released HOPE in 2014 it would not be the book you hold in your hands today. It would have been good, but not the book I was capable of writing because it would not have included as many of my personally written quotes. The original content was more inclusive of my favorite quotes written by other authors. This version is written more from my heart than from my mind. I share mostly my own quotes written by me and several of my favorite scriptures. I added a few quotes written by one of my sons. He writes under the name Nick Nova.

I encourage you to utilize HOPE, not only for encouragement, but as a journal; the pages are not numbered for that purpose. Use colorful markers to highlight your favorite sections. Place sticky notes inside the pages to add your comments. Be sure to use the empty space on each page to express your thoughts in real time. I always enjoy reading the

HOPE for the Next Step

notes I write in my Bible and in my inspirational books. I hope you will too.

HOPE for the Next Step

January 01

Always remember, you are unique, talented, and as successful and happy as you give yourself permission to be. So, today and everyday give yourself permission to be you, EXTRAORDINARILY Amazing.

HOPE for the Next Step

January 02

He cuts off every branch in me that bears no fruit, while every branch that does bear fruit he prunes so that it will be even more fruitful.
John 15:2

Purging is sometimes painful physically, financially, and spiritually, but always necessary for us to become authentically successful in all areas of our lives. It may not feel good going through, but on the other side of change and growth is always beauty. Ask any butterfly or 15-carat princess cut diamond ring!

HOPE for the Next Step

January 03

Failure is never an option, nor is making excuses. The great and successful among us live in the "No Excuse Zone" daily. Say this out loud, "Today, no matter what, I will not make any excuses or give up on my dreams."

HOPE for the Next Step

January 04

Faith is my superpower and I am "Powered by Faith."

We should wake up every day praising our Lord and Savior by continuing to pursue our purpose and being willing to be a blessing to others!
You are a winner!

HOPE for the Next Step

January 05

I will instruct you and teach you the way you should go; I will counsel you with my loving eye on you.

Psalm 32:8

This is great news. This means we do not have to figure things out all by ourselves. The blueprint is available for us 24 hours a day, 7 days a week. All we have to do is read the blueprint and apply the teachings in our daily lives.

HOPE for the Next Step

January 06

Even on your difficult days, you have so much to smile about!

On the days when you feel a little melancholy just remind yourself that even the word melancholy ends with the word holy. We have so much to appreciate in our lives. Sometimes we just need a reminder.

HOPE for the Next Step

January 07

The lips of the righteous nourish many, but fools die for lack of sense. The blessing of the LORD brings wealth, without painful toil for it. A fool finds pleasure in wicked schemes, but a person of understanding delights in wisdom.

Proverbs 10:21-23

HOPE for the Next Step

January 08

This journey called life is all about what you make it! What you put into anything is exactly what you will get out of it, nothing more and nothing less. This is how it works: average in, average out, negativity and complaining in, negativity and complaining out, excellence in, excellence out.

HOPE for the Next Step

January 09

Have you heard the saying, "junk-in junk-out?" This statement applies to our spiritual lives as well. Whatever you allow in, such as negative thoughts and bad words, if you make a habit of this, these things will be reflected in your thoughts and in the words, you speak. Thinking positive thoughts and speaking positive words can help transform your life when combined with corresponding actions.

HOPE for the Next Step

January 10

Just go out there and do what
you've got to do.

Martina Navratilova

Do not be distracted today. Keep
the faith in your dreams strong.

HOPE for the Next Step

January 11

Lord, whatever today brings, give me the strength to keep holding on to You.

Mark Collins

HOPE for the Next Step

January 12

To live a life of success, integrity, and prosperity, you should include the willingness to talk about the good and the bad. This equates to sharing your stories of overcoming triumphs and fears to help inspire others to hang in there.

HOPE for the Next Step

January 13

In 2 Kings chapter 4, God's word tells of a widow who was down to her last amount of oil. The prophet tells her to go into the village and collect as many empty jars as she can. She does this, and the oil does not run out until the last jar is filled. For me, this means that as long as I am a willing vessel the Lord will continue to pour into me. Our jars overflow. He gives the provisions to complete the work He calls us to do. Do not run out of goals/jars. For the Lord delights in giving us blessings and pouring oil into all of us every time we need it.

HOPE for the Next Step

January 14

On the days and during those moments when you do not want to work on your goals, always remind yourself of your "Why." The reason you began the work, the book, the business, the relationship.

Before you throw it all away because of one day or moment of feeling overwhelmed, not good enough, discouraged, or under-appreciated, remember the "Why." If you do not quit, there is success and fulfillment on the other side.

HOPE for the Next Step

January 15

The art of being wise is knowing what to overlook.

William James

Our goal should not be to win every argument. It is always important to be sensitive to another's point of view.

HOPE for the Next Step

January 16

The greatest natural resource in
the world is the spirit that resides
in every unstoppable person.

Cynthia Kersey

HOPE for the Next Step

January 17

The major reason for setting a goal is what it makes of you to accomplish it. What it makes of you will always be the far greater value than what you get.

Jim Rohn

HOPE for the Next Step

January 18

The value we place on something is in direct proportion to the amount of time we're willing to wait for it.

Priscilla Shirer

HOPE for the Next Step

January 19

Then you will have success, if you are careful to observe the decrees and laws that the LORD gave Moses for Israel. Be strong and courageous. Do not be afraid or discouraged.

1 Chronicles 22:13

HOPE for the Next Step

January 20

Here is some liberating information. There is no box! Your imagination holds your limitations! Expand your imagination, decrease your limitations to success and overflow. Today be BOLD! Be unapologetically You.

HOPE for the Next Step

January 21

There is no quality I would rather have, or be thought to have, than gratitude. It is not only the greatest virtue; it is the mother of all the rest.

Cicero

HOPE for the Next Step

January 22

To live is the rarest thing in the world. Most people exist, that is all.

Oscar Wilde

Here is my question to you. Is going through the same exact routines day in and day out really living? Are you living life or merely existing?

HOPE for the Next Step

January 23

> Try not to become a man of
> success but a man of value.
>
> Albert Einstein

My prayer for you today is that in
your pursuit of success, you will
always remember character is more
valuable than material things.

HOPE for the Next Step

January 24

We are what we repeatedly do.
Excellence, therefore, is not an act
but a habit.

Aristotle

HOPE for the Next Step

January 25

A lot of my best lessons learned about forgiveness and trust were taught to me by my children. They taught me if you pray for a blessing, then you your actions should be in line with your prayers.

HOPE for the Next Step

January 26

A mountain (problem) in your way means it is time to go around it, climb it, or tell it to get out of your way. It should not be used as an excuse to do nothing. You have Mountain Moving Power. It starts with making the command.

HOPE for the Next Step

January 27

Our divine purpose is higher than anything we could imagine. It is more powerful than we would have known to reach for or pray for.

Our purpose is so big that if God had not poured it into our spirit, we would still be searching into eternity. Our divine purpose will always be bigger and better than anything we could ever dream. It is, however, not out of our reach. All we have to do is continually seek God. He will always guide us!

HOPE for the Next Step

January 28

All that is gold does not glitter. Not all those who wander are lost. The old that is strong does not wither. Deep roots are not reached by the frost.

J.R.R.

HOPE for the Next Step

January 29

May I forever remember that all those nights I cried brought me closer to God. For in the midnight hour, You, alone comforted me. That's great proof that Abba Father cares and His love is never-ending.

HOPE for the Next Step

January 30

God is an uncommon friend. He can be trusted with your darkest secrets and your biggest dreams and love you unconditionally! He will never share your secrets or remind you of your mistakes. He will not deny you of the dreams that He placed in your heart.

HOPE for the Next Step

January 31

And do not neglect doing good and sharing, for with such sacrifices God is pleased.

Hebrews 13:16

HOPE for the Next Step

February 01

And He that sat upon the throne
said, Behold, I make all things new.

Revelation 21:5

HOPE for the Next Step

February 02

If the song that is in your heart is bringing you down, change the song or change the lyrics! If you do not know all of the words, do like I do and make them up as you go.

HOPE for the Next Step

February 03

And in thee shall all families of the earth be blessed.

Genesis 12:3

You are important. You were born to make a positive impact in this world. You have everything you need. Never lose your hope.

HOPE for the Next Step

February 04

And the King will say, "I tell you the truth, when you did it to one of the least of these my brothers and sisters, you were doing it to me."

Matthew 25:40

HOPE for the Next Step

February 05

Any time and money spent on education, following your dreams, helping others, or preparation for such things, should never be considered as wasted time or wasted money.

HOPE for the Next Step

February 06

Anything less than your absolute best in anything is not good enough. Anything short of your absolute best is UNACCEPTABLE. As talented as you are, you better get a grip. Your success is waiting on you. It is yours for the taking. Go get it. There is Greatness in your DNA. You are so loved.

HOPE for the Next Step

February 07

At the end of each day, play back the tapes of your performance. The results should either applaud you or prod you.

Jim Rohn

HOPE for the Next Step

February 08

Today, be excited because you are filled with the potential to be great every day. You are filled with greatness. You will be blessed with endless opportunities, even enough to be a blessing to others.

HOPE for the Next Step

February 09

You are an original. Your past, present, and future is like none other. With each experience you become more of the amazing person you were created to become. Each day ask the tough questions, embrace the answers, and trust your way.

HOPE for the Next Step

February 10

Be grateful for delays and late starts, for they could be the protection from an unknown and unseen danger up ahead. At the very least, take the extra time to be thankful.

HOPE for the Next Step

February 11

Be openhanded toward your brothers and toward the poor and the needy in your land.

Deuteronomy 15:11

HOPE for the Next Step

February 12

Behold I will do a new thing; now it shall spring forth.

Isaiah 43:19

Today, instead of stressing and complaining over a late start, being delayed by a flat tire, can't find the keys again, or traffic is stalled again, be grateful for the protection and rest. There is always a reason. Sometimes it is an opportunity for better time management. Sometimes it's just another out of your control moment. Use it wisely.

HOPE for the Next Step

February 13

Be thankful for lessons learned
from trials and tribulations, for
sometimes the pain and grief they
cause will lead the way to peace
when you trust in His care.

HOPE for the Next Step

February 14

Be happy for the jobs you did not get, for the friends who walked away, the car loans you were denied, the people who did not ask you out, and the events you were unable to attend.

There is always a reason. Sometimes it is revealed to us, and sometimes it is not. However, God's will is always for our good.

HOPE for the Next Step

February 15

Before you try to solve a friend's problem, be sure to listen more than you speak and always pray for the best response to give.

HOPE for the Next Step

February 16

Being deeply loved by someone
gives you strength, while loving
someone deeply gives you courage.

Lao Tzu

HOPE for the Next Step

February 17

Being totally dependent on the Lord is not a weakness; it is a strength few of us willingly possess. Lord, my desire is to be weak in your strength.

HOPE for the Next Step

February 18

If only we would learn to believe in our heart that everything will be all right, and release the control of the outcome, then we can know and experience the joy of walking in peace more often.

HOPE for the Next Step

February 19

> But forget all that—it is nothing compared to what I am going to do. For I am about to do something new... See, I have already begun! Do you not see it? I will make a pathway through the wilderness. I will create rivers in the dry wasteland.
>
> Isaiah 43:18-19

HOPE for the Next Step

February 20

By the power vested in me, I now pronounce me healthy, wealthy, a blessing to many, and a faithful servant of my Father.

HOPE for the Next Step

February 21

Today, call, text, or email someone that you have been thinking about lately but have not talked to or seen in a while. Take the time to say hello. It can bless them and you too.

HOPE for the Next Step

February 22

Can miles truly separate you from friends? If you want to be with someone you love, aren't you already there?

Richard Bach

HOPE for the Next Step

February 23

Change, trials, challenges, and obstacles help us grow to illumination and enlightenment. We become a beacon of light, so others may be led to Him, the source of pure light.

HOPE for the Next Step

February 24

Changes in our lives are inevitable, yet, our unwavering trust in God is always more powerful. Trusting His plan helps us to adapt and accept the changes that often lead to better. Embrace change. It is a good thing.

HOPE for the Next Step

February 25

Morning checklist for having an amazing day:

Positive thoughts. Check.

BIG Dreams. Check.

Plan of action. Check.

Prayers. Check.

Told the people I love that I love them. Check.

All right, time to go to work. Laser beam focused and a made-up mind! Check.

HOPE for the Next Step

February 26

Choose to be known for counting your blessings instead of for complaining about someone else's blessings. Being genuinely happy when someone else is blessed can open the door for your blessings to find you.

HOPE for the Next Step

February 27

Each day embrace and love all that you are so that you can become all you were created to be. You are loving, kind, smart, successful, and a valued, contributing member of society.

HOPE for the Next Step

February 28

Come to Him in prayer as a child searching, asking, and trusting that He knows and will always give you His best.

HOPE for the Next Step

March 01

Comparing yourself to someone else is wasted time. It will only produce two outcomes: pity or pride. Love and accept yourself. Pray to see yourself as God sees you.

HOPE for the Next Step

March 02

Concentrating on what you do not have leads to discontentment. Concentrating on all you do have brings joy and a grateful heart.

HOPE for the Next Step

March 03

Courage is not moving forward in the absence of fear. Courage is moving forward in spite of your fears. Today, Believe in your abilities. Be courageous. You can do it. I know you can!

HOPE for the Next Step

March 04

Discipline from the heart can soothe a hurt caused by a bad decision. When things do not happen the way you planned, speak kindness over yourself, not blame. You can then start over from a place of strength and wisdom.

HOPE for the Next Step

March 05

Do not allow life's circumstances to cause you to give up on your dreams. Use them to motivate you to move toward your destiny with more determination and faith.

HOPE for the Next Step

March 06

Do not be swayed by another person's limitation to believe in the impossible. Trust that your belief in the impossible opens the door for the "It is-possible" to happen for you.

HOPE for the Next Step

March 07

Do not let someone's bad attitude or negative behavior towards you excuse you from your excellence. Always react from a place of calmness, wisdom, and love. You may even have to step away from the situation for a moment or two, or a day or two, before responding.

HOPE for the Next Step

March 08

Do not become discouraged when people are not cheering for your dreams. I encourage you to use this as inspiration to work smarter to make your dream a reality. Then it doesn't matter if they cheer or not because your own Cheer is all that really counts!

HOPE for the Next Step

March 09

Another gentle reminder: Operate your life in the No More Excuses zone! Because, in the wonderful words of my Dad, "Where there is a committed will, there's always a way!"

HOPE for the Next Step

March 10

Be encouraged; trouble does not last always. Hold on. Be strong! God will bring you through this too! Be reminded of His past record. He has not, and never will leave us nor forsake us.

HOPE for the Next Step

March 11

Do not join an easy crowd; you won't grow. Go where the expectations and the demands to perform are high.

Jim Rohn

HOPE for the Next Step

March 12

Do not take your good health for granted. Exercise your right to build a temple worthy of the Spirit within.

HOPE for the Next Step

March 13

Do not wish for another person's life. You have your own to live. Just like the millions of stars in the sky, your light is bright to someone, too.

HOPE for the Next Step

March 14

Dream BIG dreams and start to encourage everyone around you to do the same. Develop and execute a plan for making your BIG dreams a BIG Reality. And then be sure to help someone else do the same.

HOPE for the Next Step

March 15

Dream big, so even if you do not get everything you want, what you get is really close to the original. And so much better than having no dream at all.

HOPE for the Next Step

March 16

Dream no small dreams for they have no power to move the hearts of men.

Johann Wolfgang von Goethe

HOPE for the Next Step

March 17

DREAMS REALLY DO COME TRUE when you do more than simply wish upon a star! You have the Power to create them. All you have to do is pray, plan, and execute your plan. Giving up is always too soon.

HOPE for the Next Step

March 18

Each day commit to becoming the positive change in your family, job, church, and community you want to see. Feeling tired is expected but quitting is never an option.

HOPE for the Next Step

March 19

Be mindful that sometimes blessings are disguised and may appear to be delayed. In time, you will see that it really was a blessing, for the prayer was not being delayed but was answered differently.

HOPE for the Next Step

March 20

Even in the midst of a storm, whether physical, mental, or spiritual, the SON is always shining. Sometimes you just have to intentionally look past the darkest cloud in your heart to really see HIM.

HOPE for the Next Step

March 21

Excellence simply means anything I must do or want to do should be done with a cheerful heart and to the best of my ability every time.

HOPE for the Next Step

March 22

Expect it to happen and it will happen: great days, dreams fulfilled, prayers answered, God's love and guidance.

HOPE for the Next Step

March 23

Father, you are the good, the goal, and the gift of all my searching. When I search for you, I always find my best self. In my best self is bliss and enlightenment showered with peace, joy, and love. I long for that place in You on earth. I see things more clearly when I look at my life, my family, my friends, and my circumstances through my heart instead of with my eyes alone.

HOPE for the Next Step

March 24

Focus on giants—you stumble.

Focus on God—your giants tumble.

Max Lucado

HOPE for the Next Step

March 25

For all the times I did not know what to say, for all the times I went left when you told me to go right, Lord, thank you for being there to make everything not just alright, but right.

HOPE for the Next Step

March 26

Faith, combined with wisdom, says, for every problem there are several solutions. Most times, just finding only one solution helps any situation.

HOPE for the Next Step

March 27

God can make the difference in your life today, no matter what you have done or where you have been. His love is overwhelming and unconditional, and His power is mighty and available. Have faith and ask Him to give you wisdom and guide you. He will do it for you.

HOPE for the Next Step

March 28

God does not show favoritism toward His children. Therefore, nor should we as parents, teachers, and leaders. His goodness and mercy are available to all. We can find joy and learn a lot from spending quality time with our youth.

Today, let's cover all children in prayer and love every day, not just our own.

HOPE for the Next Step

March 29

To reach and embrace a place of contentment, be grateful, everyday. Enough said. How great is our God? Say it with me. "How great, how great is our God."

HOPE for the Next Step

March 30

As one season ends, another one always begins. To experience continual peace and joy, be excited about endless possibilities and opportunities that each day brings. Make better decisions, have patience, forgive and be forgiven, and do more to help others each day.

HOPE for the Next Step

March 31

God is more than capable of doing His will without our help. I know this for a fact because I have tried to help Him many times. God loves me best. He knows everything, I mean everything about me, and He loves me anyway. WOW! That's love. He loves me better than I love myself. He will never ever give up on me. He loves you too!

HOPE for the Next Step

April 01

God's capacity to bless us is limitless. However, our capacity to receive is based on our capacity to believe, which is sometimes covered with doubt and disbelief. Today, and every day, I choose to have unlimited faith to receive God's best for me and my family.

HOPE for the Next Step

April 02

God's word is a constant reminder and a beacon of encouragement that after all I have done and been through, His love covers me and gives me peace and joy.

HOPE for the Next Step

April 03

H.O.P.E. = Having Outstanding Purpose Everyday

I want to be a blessing to someone each day. May the things I accomplish today enrich the lives of others and my life as well.

HOPE for the Next Step

April 04

Hang in there. Do not think about giving up. Give it another try. You might not figure out how to do it until you learn 772 ways how not to do it. Lessons learned are priceless.

HOPE for the Next Step

April 05

Have you ever danced in the rain? I mean literally. My sons and I enjoy dancing in the rain together. Did we get soaked? Yes, and were we the only ones in our neighborhood outside in the street dancing in the rain? Yes. Priceless and majestic! Memorable and joy filled!

I invite you to always find the joy; it is always there. Sometimes you must create the moments that give you joy. I have learned many times that simple things in life really do mean the most.

HOPE for the Next Step

April 06

Have you ever had a day when you woke up, said your prayers, and meditated on the Word and then you felt like today was going to be extra amazing? Did you believe that something wonderful was going to happen in your life, especially today? Well, I have that feeling. "I feel my help coming," as my grandmother would say. I am going to praise Him in advance. Feel free to join in. Come on and Praise Him in advance.

HOPE for the Next Step

April 07

Be intentional with your faith today. He can take away all your doubts. His Word gives you the answers and the proof. All you have to do is combine your faith with good works just as the Word encourages us to do. Faith alone does not make it happen nor does it work alone.

HOPE for the Next Step

April 08

Who redeems your life from the pit
and crowns you with love and
compassion,
who satisfies your desires with
good things
so that your youth is
renewed like the eagle's.

Psalm 103:4-5

HOPE for the Next Step

April 09

The Lord looked beyond my faults and He saw my needs. That's what unconditional love looks and feels like.

I'm singing, "I'm so glad Jesus loves me, I'm so glad Jesus loves me, I'm so glad Jesus loves me, Glory Hallelujah, Jesus really does love me."

HOPE for the Next Step

April 10

…and to know this love that surpasses knowledge—that you may be filled to the measure of all the fullness of God.

Now to him who is able to do immeasurably more than all we ask or imagine, according to his power that is at work within us, to him be glory in the church and in Christ Jesus throughout all generations, forever and ever. Amen.

Ephesians 3:19-21

I love this reassurance. Whenever you feel a little down, remind yourself of this one promise.

HOPE for the Next Step

April 11

Helplessness is one prayer away from becoming Hopefulness. Have faith that your prayers will be heard and answered. Pray out loud what is on your heart. Be honest with yourself and God. He can handle any problem.

HOPE for the Next Step

April 12

She watches over the affairs of her household and does not eat the bread of idleness.
Her children arise and call her blessed; her husband also, and he praises her: Many women do noble things, but you surpass them all.

Proverbs 31:27-29

HOPE for the Next Step

April 13

Here is an easy secret to creating and living the life you desire:

Today, start planting the things, thoughts, and treasures that you want to harvest tomorrow. For instance when you want to grow honey crisp apples, you plant a honey crisp apple seed not a tomato seed.

HOPE for the Next Step

April 14

How do we love a child, a friend, or spouse who disappoints and sometimes ignores us? Just ask our heavenly Father. He always loves us with a forgiving and loving heart, and gives us corrections for our transgressions, but He never ever withholds His love. This is the perfect example of great parenting and healthy relationships.

HOPE for the Next Step

April 15

How much does a dream cost? More than you will ever know unless you pursue your heart's desires. Dreams require us to change. Dreams ask and demand our best self. Dreams may ask us to make sacrifices of the things and people we love. However, the promise is that every person, place, and thing needed for the fulfillment of our dreams will always be made available in perfect timing. The cost of our dreams is huge and sacrificial, however, the reward and the reality of fulfilling the dream is priceless.

HOPE for the Next Step

April 16

I always wanted to be somebody, but now I realize I should have been more specific.

Lily Tomlin

Choose to be your best self, embrace your unique personality because everyone else's is taken. The world does not need another duplication of your favorite celebrity, athlete, or teacher. The world needs the authentic you.

HOPE for the Next Step

April 17

I am grateful for this day. I will cherish the chance to live another day. I will use this day to help someone. I will forgive myself and others of past hurts.

I will right a wrong and sing my favorite song out loud. I will not waste this day by focusing on the things that bring me sadness. I will use my time more wisely because I am grateful for this day.

HOPE for the Next Step

April 18

I am in a deep praise and worship mood. I am relying on HIS promises. I am not concentrating on any problems. My joy comes from knowing Jesus will work it out. Every day, I choose to walk in peace and victory!

HOPE for the Next Step

April 19

I opt out of all invitations to participate in any form of negativity and gossip, my own invitations and those of others.

Here is my standing RSVP for those types of invites:

I cannot waste my time attending "Pity's Party" ever again.

Please feel free to use my standard RSVP for any future invitations you get to "Pity Parties". I will ONLY accept invitations to Inspirational, Celebratory, and Solution oriented parties!

HOPE for the Next Step

April 20

I am praying that we are next in line for having our biggest prayer answered. I pray the solution to our challenge is revealed today.

This day is going to be simply amazing. Expect it. Watch for it. Enjoy it.

HOPE for the Next Step

April 21

I am praying, waiting, and expecting the impossible to happen in my life every day. I also pray this prayer for my family, friends, and neighbors.

I encourage you to pray too.

HOPE for the Next Step

April 22

I am so grateful for God's peace, His love, and the joy that He gives so freely to all who ask. His grace is Amazing. I am so in love with Him.

Be in love today. Love the people in your life. Love the sunshine, rain, flowers, weeds, and trees. Be in love with you.

HOPE for the Next Step

April 23

If the door opens that you have been praying for, wishing for, and hoping for, would you be READY? Are you preparing yourself or simply wishing on a star?

Preparation + Persistence + Opportunity can kick the DREAM door wide open! While you are waiting, please PREPARE. Whether it is for a husband, wife, job, promotion, children, fame and fortune, you must be READY!

HOPE for the Next Step

April 24

Have you ever wondered why, when your eyes are newly opened to new visions and dreams for next level pursuits, current things, which were once deemed great and new, now seem only average?

The answer is ascension. Now my eyes are wide open watching for the New to be revealed through that which was once good.

HOPE for the Next Step

April 25

I believe and receive what God's Word says about me. I am uniquely and divinely made for a purpose on purpose.

No matter what the circumstances are currently or what they used to be like years ago, your value is not determined by your past. You are priceless. Your life matters to this world.

HOPE for the Next Step

April 26

On days when you feel like you do not have enough, feel good enough or strong enough, let me remind you of who you really are:

"But you are a chosen people, a royal priesthood, a holy nation, God's special possession, that you may declare the praises of him who called you out of darkness into his wonderful light."

1 Peter 2:9

HOPE for the Next Step

April 27

Lord, we can remain calm in stressful situations because of your peace that you give so freely that surpasses all understanding. We are surrounded by peace.

HOPE for the Next Step

April 28

Today, say out loud; I feel a Promotion coming on. I am walking into a season of abundance!

Pray this same affirmation in the lives of others too. We will pray the same for you. I hope you are ready!

HOPE for the Next Step

April 29

Because Sometimes Sunday Morning Ain't Easy™

I have decided that instead of asking God to make my life easy all the time, I will pray for more wisdom, knowledge, and understanding.

What a difference this new prospective will make in my life and in the lives of those I love.

HOPE for the Next Step

April 30

I have learned to NOT try to solve a spiritual problem with intellect alone. I have also learned that you cannot soothe spiritual hunger with material possessions.

For only God's wisdom, love, peace, grace, and mercy can comfort and heal all things.

HOPE for the Next Step

May 01

I have learned sometimes your blessings will not necessarily come from the people you helped and supported; but from someone you have done nothing for at all. However, your blessings will come! This principle is simply amazing and true. God has His ways, and I love Him and His ways.

HOPE for the Next Step

May 02

But remember the LORD your God, for it is he who gives you the ability to produce wealth, and so confirms his covenant, which he swore to your ancestors, as it is today.

Deuteronomy 8:18

What a mighty God we serve. I embrace my billionaire mindset! I create and support Kingdom initiatives, businesses, and events. I will build houses and successful schools. I wholeheartedly support those that are enriching the lives of our youth and seniors.

HOPE for the Next Step

May 03

When you know that your dreams are gifts from God, there is no need to worry and try to force things to happen. Relax and spend your time praising God for the physical manifestation while you work in faith.

HOPE for the Next Step

May 04

I will lift up my eyes unto the hills.
Where does my help come from?
My help comes from the Lord, the
Maker of heaven and earth.

Psalm 121:1-2

HOPE for the Next Step

May 05

We should celebrate life more. There is no greater time than the present. I invite you to do the same. Make a list of all the things, people, and places that bring you joy and celebrate their existence.

HOPE for the Next Step

May 06

I pray today that my need and desire to understand why some things happen will be cast out by the faith I have in God. May I truly embrace fully, by faith, God's plan for me daily.

HOPE for the Next Step

May 07

May any plans I have made for today that are misaligned with the Father's will for me, come into full alignment with His will. Lord, I cast aside my will right now and forever. I embrace Your will for me.

HOPE for the Next Step

May 08

My prayer today, and every day, is that when people see me, they see goodness and mercy. I pray that when I speak, people will hear goodness and mercy. I pray that the way I live will lead others to God's Light, goodness, and mercy. It is not about me. It is always about His goodness and mercy.

HOPE for the Next Step

May 09

When we continually live in our comfort zones we are denying our destiny daily. Step outside your comfort zone to see a whole new world. It is beautiful on the outside.

HOPE for the Next Step

May 10

May I be filled with the wisdom to know the divine timing of when to stay and when to leave. May I know when to press my way forward and when to stand still. May I always know whether to respond with words or with my silence.

HOPE for the Next Step

May 11

May I always be reminded not to invite others to my pity parties unless I am asking for solutions. May I have the wisdom and strength to opt out of invitations of others if all they are going to do is complain the entire time without any plan or desire of overcoming in sight. May we always remember that we are all called to be salt and light, especially when we feel the opposite.

HOPE for the Next Step

May 12

My mama was truly "the man." She taught us to be our own boss and how to use adversity to our advantage. I do not know how she managed. When people find out she raised me and my four brothers to be who we are today they are awestruck. She taught us how to smile in the face of adversity; even after she lost one of us.

"Rest in Heaven, Brandon Maurice McNary" 1983-1999

Nick Nova, spoken word artist

HOPE for the Next Step

May 13

I will find a reason to celebrate every day. Each day is filled with good and perfect gifts. I have comfort knowing we always win, if we do not quit.

HOPE for the Next Step

May 14

A good fail-proof remedy when I need to lift my spirit is to find a way to help someone in need. This works every time. Decide to be a blessing to someone today.

HOPE for the Next Step

May 15

Today is the sum of all previous thoughts, beliefs, and actions. We have the power to create the life we want based on using the incredible power within us.

HOPE for the Next Step

May 16

If someone has done you wrong,
do not repay them with a wrong.

Romans 12:17

Do not let someone bring you down to their level. You are an overcomer!

HOPE for the Next Step

May 17

If you go looking for a friend,
you're going to find they're very
scarce. If you go out to be a friend,
you'll find them everywhere.

Zig Ziglar

HOPE for the Next Step

May 18

In order to be truly successful, you must give first, be a blessing first, and help someone else first. The adage, giver's gain is true.

HOPE for the Next Step

May 19

In order to be used for the glory of God, have a willing heart and a desire to be a reflection of His goodness.

HOPE for the Next Step

May 20

To succeed, you MUST Stay Focused and Stick to the original plan for your DREAM! It will unveil exactly like it was given in the VISION if you do not water the dream down. Faith is the KEY. Do not DETOUR from the dream's original blueprint.

HOPE for the Next Step

May 21

In Your Presence is where I long to be. For it is in Your Presence that I am a better me. Our truest and highest form of authenticity exists and is revealed to us while in His presence.

HOPE for the Next Step

May 22

Today I will not complain to my friends and family about any problems. Today I will pray for wisdom and solutions. I will focus my attention on all that is right in my life while creating a plan to solve the problem based on newfound wisdom and logic.

HOPE for the Next Step

May 23

Instead of staying up all night worrying about a person or a particular problem, say your prayers and go to sleep. Trust God to handle any and every problem that comes your way. He will direct you. For He neither sleeps not slumbers. No problem is too big for Him to solve.

HOPE for the Next Step

May 24

Pray for God to give you discernment, wisdom, and forgiveness. Ask him to give you the strength to stop complaining and worrying. Complaining and worrying are joy busters. Having faith and trust creates more joy.

HOPE for the Next Step

May 25

Stop wishing for someone else's life. Pray to be more thankful for yours and to live it well. Chances are someone is wishing for your life. They, too, should pray and be thankful for their own life. You can only live your own life. Remember, you have the power to make your life awesome.

HOPE for the Next Step

May 26

When planning to succeed in life or business, it has been said that the hard part is getting started, but do not let that stop you. Right behind the hard part of starting is the reward of having started. And greater is the reward of finishing.

HOPE for the Next Step

May 27

It is confirmed! The favor of God is upon me. He has ordered my steps and answered my prayers! I am so grateful and inspired by all who brave their own personal storms by faith.

HOPE for the Next Step

May 28

It is so amazing and refreshing that He knows everything about us, including our faults and future mistakes; yet He loves us better than anyone in this world. This insurance and assurance are priceless.

HOPE for the Next Step

May 29

It is so energizing to know that God never takes vacation days, holidays, or sick days. He does not call in if the weather is good or bad. He is always on the job. That's amazing love and eternal protection.

HOPE for the Next Step

May 30

It may seem as if those who hurt you have some kind of power over you. That may be true, until you forgive them. Forgiveness restores the power back to you. Forgive and receive your power back today. Forgiveness is not about the other person, it is about you.

HOPE for the Next Step

May 31

I've learned from experience that which you freely give away, comes back to you. So, always give your best!

HOPE for the Next Step

June 01

One of the best ways to stop worrying about someone, or something, is to pray, because it is not possible to pray and worry at the same time.

HOPE for the Next Step

June 02

Just like there are multiple ways to reach a destination, or cook chicken, eggs, and potatoes, there are multiple ways to be grateful. Pray, praise, help others, worship, and always be kind.

HOPE for the Next Step

June 03

Just think, if we had given up on our dreams and potential a long time ago, we would not be where we are today with endless possibilities and opportunities.

HOPE for the Next Step

June 04

Put into practice what you learned
and received from me, both from
my words and from my actions.
And the God who gives us peace
will be with you.

Philippians 4:9

HOPE for the Next Step

June 05

When it looks as if your dream is not going to happen, and you feel all alone, keep praying for the physical manifestation of your prayers. Do not stop praying until your prayer seamlessly transitions into a song of continual praise. The manifestation may be delayed or denied, but your heart and soul will feel better.

HOPE for the Next Step

June 06

Let all that I am praise the Lord;
may I never forget the good things
he does for me.

Psalm 103:2

HOPE for the Next Step

June 07

Life is a process of becoming, a combination of states we have to go through. Where people fail is that they wish to elect a state and remain in it. This is a kind of death.

Anais Nin

HOPE for the Next Step

June 08

Life is like riding a bicycle. To keep your balance, you must keep moving.

Albert Einstein

If you fall stand up, dust yourself off and continue pursuing your purpose. Each step you take, gets you closer to the manifestation you desire.

HOPE for the Next Step

June 09

Life is not just what happens to you. Life is inclusive of everything you experience, combined with the attitude you presented. Your attitude does count. It is sometimes remembered more than the actual experience.

HOPE for the Next Step

June 10

Life is to be lived. It is not a spectator sport! Get in the GAME. Stop all the whining and complaining. Find something in your life right now to be grateful for. You cannot be thankful and whiny at the same time.

Sometimes life is not easy but let me tell you it is definitely worth living. Goal for today: LIVE on purpose with gratitude and defined actions!

HOPE for the Next Step

June 11

Even if the day is filled with liquid sunshine, and a few dark clouds, choose to find your happy place within your heart. Today, help make someone's day great.

Money is not the only ideal gift, a kind word, quality time, or a prayer for them can brighten a day.

So, smile at the next person you see and say, "Have a great day!"

HOPE for the Next Step

June 12

Sometimes it changes our perspective, when we simply apologize to ourselves for the times we felt let down, abandoned, and alone. Love yourself totally and completely. Embrace everything about you. Stand in front of the mirror and say: "I love you." Let your smile reach your eyes, your heart, and your soul. This exercise can brighten even the toughest day.

HOPE for the Next Step

June 13

Today, be determined to listen twice as much than you speak. Give more than you take. Smile instead of frown, no matter what. Understand more than trying to prove your point. Give compliments instead of complaining.

HOPE for the Next Step

June 14

Living a life filled with purpose and grace brings unspeakable joy, peace that surpasses your understanding, and so many eternal rewards. Be determined to live your life on purpose and with purpose. Encourage others to do the same.

HOPE for the Next Step

June 15

Lord, I pray that you will soften the hearts and comfort those whom I have offended. I ask for their forgiveness.

As you have forgiven me, I pray that I will remember to forgive myself and others too.

HOPE for the Next Step

June 16

Lord, pour your light into me so that I may help lead others to you. I am grateful for the grace and understanding you freely give to me.

May I freely give that same grace and understanding to others; especially when what I really want to do is to give them the silent treatment.

HOPE for the Next Step

June 17

Lord, when my decisions and actions are counterproductive to Your will, please gently remind me of Your will. Moreover, may I auto correct my course to your will.

HOPE for the Next Step

June 18

Lord, as much as I love and want to protect my children, I know without any doubt that You love them best, and you will protect them better.

I surrender my plans for them to you, God. I freely give them back to your care.

HOPE for the Next Step

June 19

Although, harder than a diamond, life is still a great time. I am always ready to fight for it with my fist balled up when it's game time.

Life is like playing organized and street basketball at the same time. Even though I frequently foul, the referee says the ball remains mine.

Nick Nova, spoken word artist

HOPE for the Next Step

June 20

Lord, help me to be a finisher like You. I pray that whatever you give my hands to do, remind me that You will always give me the strength and the wisdom to complete.

Lord, bless me with a brighter perspective today. Help my eyes and heart to focus on You.

HOPE for the Next Step

June 21

Today I seek your wisdom and strength to know your perfect timing. I pray that I will not get ahead of You nor lag behind Your plan for me today.

HOPE for the Next Step

June 22

Whether people love it, like it, or leave it, I am obligated to be me.

Being who others want me to be is not an option. I answer only to one POWER. The power of God. And it is so liberating. I highly recommend it. Someday, I want to hear the Father say, 'Well done, my good and faithful servant, in you I am well pleased!' This creates a standard of excellence for my life and service.

HOPE for the Next Step

June 23

When it comes to living my life in an excellent way, I will never give up on my dreams, I will always look ahead, always speak positive, and do all I can to please only HIM. So, each day you can be sure that I am living the life I dream about, and I am encouraging others to do the same.

HOPE for the Next Step

June 24

Make sure the people you love, not only hear you say it, but may they see and feel your love in all you do, every day. Especially on the days when you feel like they do not appreciate your love.

HOPE for the Next Step

June 25

May I never be fooled by the luster and deception of pride and selfish-sufficiency. May I always rely on Your everlasting help. For I can do nothing without You, Father God.

HOPE for the Next Step

June 26

May I never become a slave to busyness. For it is in my times of stillness and quietness that my spirit connects with and hears the Lord better.

HOPE for the Next Step

June 27

I love God. He made a way when traffic was at a standstill. He made a diamond out of a lump of coal that was stranded in a landfill.

When it seemed as if the devil had the upper hand, he made my hands still; stepped in front, told Satan be gone my son can't be touched.

Nick Nova, spoken word artist

HOPE for the Next Step

June 28

May your cup always overflow with peace, love, gratitude, and joy. Everything else will fall in place.

May the way I live my life always line up with God's purpose for my life and please him daily.

HOPE for the Next Step

June 29

Lord, may Your unique plans for me, my family, and my friends, always supersede the plans we have made on our own.

HOPE for the Next Step

June 30

I speak to the Mountain of frustration, poverty, and sickness: "Get out of my way, right NOW."

I believe and expect that today is a Greater Day filled with peace, wealth, and good health, in the mighty name of Jesus, and it is so.

HOPE for the Next Step

July 01

I am happy knowing that My Father owns everything! There is no lack in my life. "Lack, you are not welcome here. I evict you and the spirit of "not enough" right now, in the name of Jesus".

Only wealth, good health, successful businesses, and mutually respectful relationships are wanted and welcomed in my life. Lord thank you for wisdom, knowledge and understanding.

HOPE for the Next Step

July 02

I am so happy my job is not to criticize or condemn others.

That's one less thing I have on my to-do-list. For this I am grateful.

HOPE for the Next Step

July 03

My daily reminder and motivation:

Jeremiah 29:11 (NLV) says, "For I know the plans that I have for you, plans for well-being, and not for trouble, to give you a future and a hope."

HOPE for the Next Step

July 04

I always travel with grace and mercy. Life is not a dress rehearsal. Everything I do today will be done in faith and without fear. When I remember this day, may the memories be filled with love, laughter, peace, and health for me, and everyone associated with me. I will bring my A-game every day, and I expect victory every time.

HOPE for the Next Step

July 05

Never allow, or accept, someone else's definition of you or your dreams. I am more than capable and equipped with the wisdom to define and live my life however I choose, based on God's Word and promises.

Your success can only be achieved or annulled by you. Stop giving your power away to a less qualified person or knock-off version of your best self. Your success is earned and defined by you.

HOPE for the Next Step

July 06

You have no excuses and no regrets when you live and walk in integrity. When you look back over your life, you should be proud, and not ashamed. Be motivated to live consistently in integrity both presently and in the future.

When you make a mistake, recalibrate, pray for forgiveness, and chart a new and improved course.

HOPE for the Next Step

July 07

Each day, I am determined to be happy and joyful, not because of my intelligence, bounty, or beauty, but because of HIS grace, mercy, and favor. I am grateful and eternally thankful for every breath and every moment!

HOPE for the Next Step

July 08

Great things do not happen without ACTION. And, of course, prayer is the key. It takes unwavering faith attached to calculated actions to unlock the door to success, wealth, and good health in life.

There is a huge difference between wishing a thing to happen and working to making a dream become a reality. You get to choose.

HOPE for the Next Step

July 09

On the days that you are distracted, dejected, or discouraged, ask for His peace. Say, 'Thank you, Father.' The circumstance may not change immediately, but your perception will change.

HOPE for the Next Step

July 10

On the days when I cannot see your hand because maybe Murphy's Law is working overtime, or there has been poor planning on my part, I will trust Your plan even more because I know I can depend on you.

HOPE for the Next Step

July 11

On the days when it feels as if your prayers are in vain, know that He always hears you. He is working it out for you. Continue to pray and believe, especially when you feel alone and as if no one cares. God is a promise keeper.

HOPE for the Next Step

July 12

One morning, as I was praying, I felt my son kneel beside me. I continued to pray and praise the Father. When I finished, I opened my eyes and looked over to see that it was my 16-year old instead of my 13-year old who does this sometimes. He continued to kneel even after I finished.

There is no better way to start my day than to witness my sons start their day with prayer. The memory of this still causes my heart to smile. Set a virtuous standard in your household.

HOPE for the Next Step

July 13

And the day came when the risk to remain tight in a bud was more painful than the risk it took to blossom.

Anais Nin

I have loved this quote for years. For some reason, it takes pain in our lives for us to grow and to move out of our comfort zones. I often wonder why this is true.

HOPE for the Next Step

July 14

Let me remind you, no matter how well thought out or strategic the plan, goal, dream or wish, nothing will happen if you do not believe it, visualize it, have faith in it, and work at it daily. You must put action to it.

And expect it to happen!

HOPE for the Next Step

July 15

Only an empty vessel can be filled. So, get rid of the things and people that bring you down, that take up space, and fill your heart with despair. Until you get rid of the useless things, you cannot fill your heart and life with people and things that can fill your heart with love, joy, peace, happiness, wealth, and purpose. Remember, Spring cleaning can happen anytime.

HOPE for the Next Step

July 16

Sometimes only in our brokenness
can we be made whole.

Pray for renewal and restoration
today for yourself and others.

HOPE for the Next Step

July 17

My desire is to always be the kind of person that does not worry about distance, time, or cost when my family and friends need me.

If ever my family or friends need me, and for reasons out of my control, I cannot get to them, may the assurance that I am praying for them be comforting until I, or others, can offer further assistance.

HOPE for the Next Step

July 18

Prayer and meditation can help you get through anything. These two are like medicine to the soul. Use them freely and often. Share them with others. The benefits are countless and priceless.

HOPE for the Next Step

July 19

Praying that this day brings you a fresh dose of hope, renewal, rejuvenation and restoration!

HOPE for the Next Step

July 20

Quitting is never an option. Give it another try. Say another prayer. Affirm out loud: "Good things are supposed to happen to me each day. Greatness is inside of me waiting to pour out onto everything I touch. I will not quit."

HOPE for the Next Step

July 21

Pray and smile often throughout the day. Think positive thoughts. Dream big dreams.

Make great things happen. Never forget to help someone along the way.

HOPE for the Next Step

July 22

Our subconscious minds have no sense of humor, play no jokes, and cannot tell the difference between reality and an imagined thought or image. What we continually think about eventually will manifest in our lives.

Sidney Madwed

HOPE for the Next Step

July 23

Reach out and touch somebody's hand, intentionally. Walk beside them for a while. Share an encouraging word. Help where you can.

We have the power to make this world a better place! I believe that we can. Say a prayer of peace today for our families, our communities, our Nation, and the entire Universe.

HOPE for the Next Step

July 24

The desire to reflect His glory
means learning to praise and trust
the Father in all circumstances.
What you reflect to the world
comes back to you.

Today, may you reflect kindness,
understanding, encouragement,
peace, and love.

HOPE for the Next Step

July 25

Rejoice, Rejoice, Rejoice in the Lord always, especially in the moments when you really do not feel like rejoicing. An offering of Praise can help you see things through God's eyes.

There is always a reason to rejoice. If you search with your heart, you will find a reason.

HOPE for the Next Step

July 26

There is purpose in everything that happens in our lives, the good and the not so good. Sometimes it is a lesson for us, and sometimes it is for us to teach others.

Even when you cannot see the good in a situation and it hurts, please trust that God is always right there. No matter how much it hurts you right now, God always takes on most of the pain. That's real love, and it softens everything you had to go through.

HOPE for the Next Step

July 27

I remind myself that when I help someone else become successful it takes nothing from me.

Matter of fact, the feeling of having helped someone is rewarding.

HOPE for the Next Step

July 28

We can rejoice, too, when we run into problems and trials, for we know that they help us develop endurance. And endurance develops strength of character, and character strengthens our confident hope of salvation.

Romans 5:3-4

HOPE for the Next Step

July 29

Follow this quick and easy "Recipe for Success and Happiness"

In your life, mix whole parts of, Seek God for the answers.

Blend in, Believe in yourself.

Add in, Follow your own dreams.

And bake at 365 days of: Help someone do the same.

HOPE for the Next Step

July 30

Seeking the wisdom of those you trust can be valuable, however, when making the final decision, it should be based on God's plan for you mixed with your own intuitiveness.

HOPE for the Next Step

July 31

Silence really is golden.

Do not dignify stupidity with your wisdom by responding to foolishness.

Silence always speaks loud and clear and triumphs when thoughtlessness is talking.

HOPE for the Next Step

August 01

Faith reassures that we will always have comfort for the tears, light when all seems dark, and relief from the pain of sickness and sorrow.

HOPE for the Next Step

August 02

Some people plant in the spring and leave in the summer. If you've signed up for a season, see it through. You do not have to stay forever, but at least stay until you see it through.

Jim Rohn

HOPE for the Next Step

August 03

Dreams! The fuel of fools. No. Dreams are real. Folly follows those who do not reach their destiny.

Some say it will never happen but there is Hope for the hopeless, saying it'll happen one day. But the remedy is Stop putting off Sunday's mission for a Monday.

Start at your current position, master patience and make your dreams a reality.

Nick Nova, spoken word artist

HOPE for the Next Step

August 04

In order to see the brightest star in the sky, you sometimes have to stretch high, tiptoe, look past the bushes and trees that block your view.

Sometimes the smallest things can block our view of the beauty in life. Do not let anything or anyone block your view of the goodness of the Lord in your life.

HOPE for the Next Step

August 05

Some days you could use a shoulder to lean on, someone to hold your hand, or a second chance due to a problem or a feeling of melancholy.

The next time you start to feel that way, offer a shoulder, a hand, or another chance to someone who needs it, too. This is a simple, yet very effective action to take to feel joy deep down in your soul.

HOPE for the Next Step

August 06

It is the genuine love in our heart that speaks louder and clearer than the words from our mouth.

I pray this is always the case when we do not know the right words to comfort or to correct ourselves and others.

HOPE for the Next Step

August 07

Overnight success takes years and years. Keep moving forward.

Do you want to know what the key to overnight success is: Never Ever Quit. Success rarely happens overnight, if ever. So, keep believing and keep working on making your dreams come true.

If you do not quit, I will see you at the top where all the stars belong. And just in case you have not heard this lately, you, my dear, are a "Super Star."

HOPE for the Next Step

August 08

Speak life today. Speak kind words over your family and friends. Speak peace and protection in your neighborhood.

Speak blessing and joy over churches, schools, and the government.

Speak success and peace in the lives of entrepreneurs and entertainers.

HOPE for the Next Step

August 09

May I continue to take the time to listen with my heart and with my soul for the answers I have been searching for in God's word.

In the stillness of the day and night, I desire for nothing but to hear from God.

HOPE for the Next Step

August 10

Today Make a Special Announcement:

I will write my answer plainly on tablets, so that a runner can carry the correct message to others. His vision is for a future time. It describes the end. If it seems slow in coming, wait patiently, and it will be fulfilled, for it will surely take place. It will not be delayed.

Habakkuk 2:2-3

HOPE for the Next Step

August 11

Stick to the original blueprint of your VISION. Do not rush it; but do not move too slowly. Do not settle for the "good thing."

Wait and seek the "God thing." Be encouraged to wait upon the Lord.

HOPE for the Next Step

August 12

Stop signing up for things that just simply interest you. When you give your word, you should feel passionate and driven to be a part of not only the process but a part of the agreed upon outcome as well. Otherwise, your commitment to things that you have no emotional attachment to at best is merely a fleeting thought.

Real commitment is concentration, plus a personal promise to see-it-through to the stated deadline and outcome.

HOPE for the Next Step

August 13

Strengthen the feeble hands,
steady the knees that give way;
say to those with fearful hearts,
"Be strong, do not fear;
your God will come,
he will come with vengeance;
with divine retribution
he will come to save you.

Isaiah 35:3-4

Find assurance in knowing that on
the days you feel too weak to
follow your dreams or to
accomplish your everyday chores,
God is a restorer. He cares about
everything that concerns us.

HOPE for the Next Step

August 14

Success never comes before having faith and doing the hard work.

Success does not enter before faith and hard work. Not even in the dictionary and certainly not in real life. We must do the work first!

HOPE for the Next Step

August 15

Sunshine or rain - same God. So, carry on with your day in faith no matter the weather.

There will always be protection and provision to complete the work you were divinely assigned.

HOPE for the Next Step

August 16

How do you overcome obstacles
and unpleasant circumstances?

Take it one day at a time and
create a plan of action. Adversity
and large tasks become more
manageable and easier when you
take things one day at a time.

HOPE for the Next Step

August 17

Take the first step, even if it is a baby step, to pursuing your purpose.

The irony is that the first step is both the most difficult and one of the most memorable steps you will ever take.

HOPE for the Next Step

August 18

Say these affirming statements out loud everyday:

I am Grateful for this day. I am grateful for my life, family, friends, church, job, business, health, my purpose, and my community.

HOPE for the Next Step

August 19

The first phase to starting something new, or walking away from a problematic situation, is usually a difficult decision to make.

However, without choosing to take the first step you will never know you can walk. Nor can you really know or discover your greatest potential.

HOPE for the Next Step

August 20

The goal is the same: life itself; and the price is the same; life itself.

James Agee

HOPE for the Next Step

August 21

The greatest form of maturity is at harvest time. This is when we must learn how to reap without complaint if the amounts are small and how to reap without apology if the amounts are big.

Jim Rohn

HOPE for the Next Step

August 22

The lifetime journey of living life with purpose begins with a lot of soul-searching, praying, taking one step, and one day at a time.

Today I invite you to decide to take one step to seek, discover, and then pursue your purpose.

And next, I encourage you to live each day fulfilling your purpose.

HOPE for the Next Step

August 23

Most days all you need to do to get through a hectic day is to smile and take some deep breaths.

On the days when you feel a little overwhelmed from work or circumstances, look in the mirror, simply smile, and whisper these words, "Thank you Jesus."

Gratitude can change your attitude and your altitude.

HOPE for the Next Step

August 24

The Bible says, be faithful over a few things.

Each day create a list of things you currently have and give thanks. Spend less time complaining about things you do not have, yet.

A delayed answered to your prayers does not mean His answer is no. Always have grateful heart each day.

HOPE for the Next Step

August 25

Then Jesus said to the disciples, "Have faith in God. I tell you the truth, you can say to this mountain, May you be lifted up and thrown into the sea, and it will happen. But you must really believe it will happen and have no doubt in your heart. I tell you, you can pray for anything, and if you believe that you've received it, it will be yours.

Mark 11:22-24

HOPE for the Next Step

August 26

Today be grateful for your WHY!

Your WHY is the reason you started a business, the reason you decided to stop a bad habit, the reason you set a goal.

Your WHY will always keep you from quitting and from making excuses. Sometimes your WHY will change, and that's okay. Just keep the faith.

HOPE for the Next Step

August 27

Then shalt thou call, and the Lord shall answer. Thou shalt cry, and He shall say, Here I am...

Isaiah 58:9

HOPE for the Next Step

August 28

There are no failures, only opportunities.

Michael V. Roberts

Failure is not the opposite nor the absence of success. Failure is just proof that you tried something different, you took a risk. And perhaps you learned what will not work, or maybe you learned a better way of doing something.

Often a failure can lead you closer to a success, than not trying at all.

HOPE for the Next Step

August 29

There are three great
characteristics of a champion:
talent, hard work, and integrity.

The greatest of these is integrity.

HOPE for the Next Step

August 30

There are your plans, plans others make for you, and then there is God's plan.

Remember, God's plan is always the best and better plan.

HOPE for the Next Step

August 31

People with focused excellence have faith and work relentlessly on their vision. Even though they see small results, they trust the vision will manifest and they do not quit.

People without focused excellence, work on a dream haphazardly and see no results, then they blame the dream, and not their lack of faith and actions. They give up, saying it was not meant to be. Choose excellence, it will keep your dreams alive!

HOPE for the Next Step

September 01

There is no greater love than that of my Father.

My desire is to love myself and others like He loves us. I am so thankful for the blueprint He freely gives us.

Because His love is ever-lasting and extravagant!

HOPE for the Next Step

September 02

There is no way around it; it takes hard work, wisdom, change, and compromise to have a great life, a healthy body, a renewed mind, and a restored soul.

You must do the work daily. The desired result will be worth all of your hard work.

HOPE for the Next Step

September 03

Pain and struggle are not always meant to stop you. Sometimes it just means something greater is on the way.

Keep praying. Keep praising. Keep believing. Keep hoping. Keep being a blessing. And watch mighty things move in your favor.

HOPE for the Next Step

September 04

This third, I will put into the fire;
I will refine them like silver
and test them like gold.
They will call on my name
and I will answer them;
I will say, 'They are my people,'
and they will say, 'The LORD is our God.'

Zechariah 13:9

There is so much power in the name of Jesus! When you can't say anything else, just say Jesus. He will direct your path. He will counsel and comfort you.

HOPE for the Next Step

September 05

Ascension in your life is a direct result of striving for excellence in all you do.

Get rid of the "that'll do" attitude. Do your best every time in every situation so that things that once seemed good are now "not good enough."

When excellence is your normal standard, joy and success are not far away.

HOPE for the Next Step

September 06

Think before you speak. Words, whether good or bad, are nonrefundable. Be intentional with your thoughts, words, and actions.

Once they are released, there is no recall button that can erase their impact whether positive or negative. Always be kind with your words.

HOPE for the Next Step

September 07

Think positive, dream big dreams, and help someone along the way.

Be spontaneous today. Do something for someone today that will enhance their day.

HOPE for the Next Step

September 08

Dreams are to be celebrated and enjoyed. If someone does not believe in your dream, do not waste your time trying to convince them.

Working persistently to make your dreams a reality is your best defense against naysayers.

HOPE for the Next Step

September 09

When we help others reach their goals, whether it is random or intentional, we benefit as well.

We receive joy in helping others and they feel joy because we helped them. Spread some joy around today.

HOPE for the Next Step

September 10

To become the man or woman you were created to be, learn to cherish every moment you get to experience on this earth.

That includes accepting the happy with the sad, the good with the bad, and the bitter with the sweet.

When you do, you will shine, shine, shine just like the millions of stars in the sky!

HOPE for the Next Step

September 11

To enjoy and to help ensure your day is good, pray often, think positive thoughts, seek to understand, and listen before you speak.

HOPE for the Next Step

September 12

Faith believes that your prayers will be answered according to what you want and what you work for in your life, and aligns with God's will.

The reward of Faith is the manifestation of what you believed before you saw it.

Trust in the power of your prayers.

Trust in the power of faith.

Trust in the power of hope.

HOPE for the Next Step

September 13

Today be impeccable with your words!

Especially when you are talking about your spouse, children, church, and your job. You create life circumstances with the words you speak.

Try changing the way you see those things you once spoke so negatively about day in and day out. Say only what you really want to manifest in your life.

Either those things will become better or your outlook will become more optimistic.

HOPE for the Next Step

September 14

He who has a WHY to live can bear most any HOW.

Friedrich Nietzsche

HOPE for the Next Step

September 15

Today begin to Seek God for the answers.

Believe in yourself. Regardless of what someone else is saying about you and your dreams.

Follow your OWN Dreams wholeheartedly and help motivate others to do the same!

HOPE for the Next Step

September 16

Today choose the high road when dealing with a difficult person or situation. Even if you are the one always taking the high road.

You may not see an immediate payoff, but someday, someone will take the high road because you showed them the way.

HOPE for the Next Step

September 17

Today I am grateful for the honor and privilege to be a mother, a grandmother, a daughter, a sister, an aunt, and a friend.

Being intentionally grateful releases endorphins and causes you to feel good all day long!

HOPE for the Next Step

September 18

Today be open to hearing new ideas. Commit to doing your best when doing something different.

At the very least, take the time to listen to your own heart beat. And fall in love with the beautiful sound of your heart beating. It is blissful.

HOPE for the Next Step

September 19

Today, I give thanks for my dad and for my mother. I give my love to them always; no matter the circumstances.

I am grateful that Love covers all things. Show special appreciation and pray for those who continue to love you unconditionally.

HOPE for the Next Step

September 20

Today, I will slow down so that I may appreciate the intoxicating smell of a flower, the beautiful sight of a newly mowed lawn, and breath-taking warmth of the sun.

Today, I will see things through the eyes of a curious child, for they see beauty through nonjudgmental eyes.

HOPE for the Next Step

September 21

Today is a great day to begin the thing you wanted to begin on yesterday to help make your dreams come true; but you let fear stop you.

"Be courageous; do that "thing" even though you feel afraid."

Use your fear to propel you to success. You can do it!

HOPE for the Next Step

September 22

Today is a new season for me. I am walking in a fresh anointing to do what I have been destined to do all my life.

Nothing is going to stop me! I was born to win!

HOPE for the Next Step

September 23

Today is a beautiful day! Be sure to spend time outdoors, walking, picnicking, singing, dancing, yard work, washing the car, chatting with neighbors, or just sit inside and be in awe of His majesty.

Be thankful!

HOPE for the Next Step

September 24

Today is the start of something GREAT!

Seek it and you shall find it. Knock and the doors shall be opened. Be grateful and thankful.

Seeing life through grateful eyes improves our outlook.

HOPE for the Next Step

September 25

One day, my son, Jacob, chose to read Psalm 117:1. When I asked him to tell me what he read, he recited Psalm 117:1 verbatim.

"O praise the LORD, all ye nations: praise him, all ye people."

Impressive. Right? Until he says he chose Psalm 117:1, because it was "short."

Honesty is always the best policy. Then he goes on to say, "Mom, it is not how much you read; it's how much you get out of what you read."

I appreciate moments like these.

HOPE for the Next Step

September 26

Today, opt out of any invitations to pout, doubt, whine, and complain.

Choose to be grateful for another day by being positive and appreciative.

HOPE for the Next Step

September 27

Today, boldly decide to become all you were created to be!

Do not waiver and do not speak unkind of your decision to follow your dreams, not even jokingly.

I will see you at the top! Yes, and Amen!

HOPE for the Next Step

September 28

Today, call, write, or send a quick text to a friend wishing them a great day.

It will make their day and it will make yours brighter, too!

HOPE for the Next Step

September 29

Today, I am reminded, passion and purpose trump position.

Meaning that, we have all we need when we live in integrity and give freely to help others. Our value is not predicated by material possessions.

Regardless of my job title, zip code, or bank account balance, I am awesome.

HOPE for the Next Step

September 30

Today, I am resting in His shadow!

Precious Moments in His presence brings peace, clarity, restoration, and joy. We should make the time to do this more often.

Find a quiet place to sit and relish in the silence and peace that will surround you.

HOPE for the Next Step

October 01

Whenever you start feeling like you are stuck or in a rut, pray for the wisdom to think differently and do things differently, and watch your life improve right in front of you. So, if your desire is to speak and be different tomorrow, be different today!

HOPE for the Next Step

October 02

A good way to get your mind off your problems, have a quality conversation with your sons, daughters, nieces or nephews and remind them how great they are.

It is a blessing to be able to listen to and inspire our future presidents, CEOs, doctors, artists, entrepreneurs, dancers, engineers, academy award winners, scientists, teachers, ministers, spiritual leaders, politicians, attorneys, truck drivers, dentists, and PR experts!

HOPE for the Next Step

October 03

Today, I will find a way to encourage myself.

No need to call anyone for help. Perhaps I will listen to my favorite songs or maybe I will read my favorite book or scripture. Or I might sit still and do nothing at all.

Whatever it takes, today I will encourage myself.

HOPE for the Next Step

October 04

Trust and believe He will supply every one of your needs! I know this for a fact. Stay in His Presence.

Remind yourself that you are a lender, not a borrower. You are the head, not the tail. You are an overcomer!

HOPE for the Next Step

October 05

Until you value yourself, you will not value your time. Until you value your time, you will not do anything with it.

M. Scott Peck

HOPE for the Next Step

October 06

Visualize every aspect of your dream in your mind. Believe with all your heart that it will become a reality.

Let that trust soak into your soul. Keep a gratitude journal. Read it often.

Expect to see the difference in your circumstances and your perception will change.

HOPE for the Next Step

October 07

After saying your prayers, meditate on having a great day. Believe that every resource you need for the day comes to you in a perfect and divine way!

Give thanks in advance for God's provisions and protection. Be thankful to be alive. Make the best out of whatever this day brings.

HOPE for the Next Step

October 08

When you believe the dream that is in your heart, your faith will be powered by the level of your belief.

You must believe in your dreams without any doubt. When you have a dream and you do not fully believe it will come true, your faith will lack the power it needs to produce the dream at the desired level.

Level up your belief!

HOPE for the Next Step

October 09

Waiting is a big part of life. Waiting produces patience. And patience can only be developed or attained by learning to wait.

When waiting becomes difficult, pray for guidance so you will know whether to be still or whether to apply action. Listen and watch for the answers to come to you.

HOPE for the Next Step

October 10

We are only limited by our agreement to embrace said limitation, but wisdom, knowledge and understanding will outperform a limitation every time.

HOPE for the Next Step

October 11

Happiness cannot be traveled to, owned, earned, worn, or consumed. Happiness is the spiritual experience of living every minute with love, grace, and gratitude.

Denis Waitley

HOPE for the Next Step

October 12

What a wonderful day! So glad I am a "go with the flow" person.

Amazing things can happen when you surrender to His will.

Today just say "Lord, I surrender all to you." It is so refreshing to lay all our burdens at His feet. What an amazing privilege we have as believers.

HOPE for the Next Step

October 13

What I know for certain is that when you are faithful and embrace a kingdom mindset, there is no such thing as coincidence.

Nothing occurs by chance, and that which seems a misfortune, is often a blessing in disguise. Let's all say "Wow" and "Amen!"

HOPE for the Next Step

> October 14

> The greatest gifts you can give
> your children are the roots of
> responsibility and the wings of
> independence.
>
> Denis Waitley

HOPE for the Next Step

October 15

That's why I take pleasure in my weaknesses, and in the insults, hardships, persecutions, and troubles that I suffer for Christ. For when I am weak, then I am strong.

II Corinthians 12:10

When doubts filled my mind, your comfort gave me renewed hope and cheer.

Psalm 94:19

HOPE for the Next Step

October 16

When I diligently searched for meaning in my life and eagerly pursued the Father's will, that's when I began to know more about me and began to embrace who I was created to become. This is freedom.

HOPE for the Next Step

October 17

When I seek His wisdom and guidance, I always learn more about me, and I feel empowered to inspire others to do the same. This act of compassion liberates all of us.

HOPE for the Next Step

October 18

When I seek the good in others, I am often reminded of the good in me. This awakens the greatness in me to be the best I can be every moment of my life.

HOPE for the Next Step

October 19

On my pilgrimage of needing to know more about God, during a time in my life when I needed Him the most, I began to know more about the woman He created me to be.

For this beautiful privilege and amazing knowledge, I am eternally thankful.

HOPE for the Next Step

October 20

When it is time to make a life altering decision, the advice of others can be valuable, however, only you can make the best decision for you by using a combination of wise counsel and your intuition. Right or wrong, it should be your decision.

This revelation is great proof that it is always good to pray for wisdom, knowledge, and understanding.

HOPE for the Next Step

October 21

When life starts to feel like a huge boulder is on your shoulders, visualize a time that was similar and remind yourself how you made it over.

If you made it through before, you can definitely do it again!

Have hope because God never fails.

HOPE for the Next Step

October 22

When negative messages take up space in your mind, send them an eviction notice immediately, and then tell yourself, "Good job."

HOPE for the Next Step

October 23

If the desire, commitment, and willingness to do all that you can to make your dreams come true exceeds the frustration of being afraid to take a chance, providence happens, greatness is revealed, and dreams manifest.

HOPE for the Next Step

October 24

Grace is the many times I doubted things would get better, and I did not give it my all. Although I struggled and stumbled, I did not fall.

HOPE for the Next Step

October 25

When the longing to pursue your purpose becomes more powerful than the fear of trying, then you will find the strength and the direction to proceed.

When the pain of being stagnant is more painful than the thought of moving forward, then you will know it is time to make a significant change or simply change your way of thinking about your circumstances. Embracing change is good.

HOPE for the Next Step

October 26

Stand your ground when someone wants to talk you out of following your dreams. Be like Nehemiah in the Bible and tell them you are doing a great work and cannot come down from the wall you are protecting and building.

The dream was put in your heart. Sometimes family and friends will not understand. Do not let their doubt cause you to give up or become distracted. Stay focused.

HOPE for the Next Step

October 27

When you begin to doubt your dreams, talk to the Father.

He created your destiny; and He alone knows exactly what you need to make your dreams a reality.

HOPE for the Next Step

October 28

The minute you commit totally to your purpose, providence shows up.

Saying yes is necessary for the release of the right resources and opportunities for your success.

Now watch all the great things start to unfold.

HOPE for the Next Step

October 29

Once you feel a nudge or a need to call someone or to do something out of the ordinary for someone, but have been putting it off, do it today.

HOPE for the Next Step

October 30

If you are feeling doubtful and depressed, simply connect with the sweet memories, of happy times, and the people that bring you joy.

Singing and dancing to your favorite song helps too!

HOPE for the Next Step

October 31

Uncertainty can cause you to feel stuck in a rut, mentally exhausted, or spiritually tired.

Here is the remedy. When you feel like standing, run. When you feel like sitting, stand. When you feel like lying down, crawl.

When you feel like you can't crawl, scoot. You have more energy than you think. Pray one more prayer. Always do a little more than you thought you could.

It is rewarding when you prove that you are stronger than you think!

HOPE for the Next Step

November 01

When you feel tired or weak, that is a sign you should plug back into your power Source.

Praying changes and restores our countenance. It connects us to the always available Power Source.

Do the work and Power UP.

HOPE for the Next Step

November 02

When you know what brings you joy, then do more of the things that bring you joy.

Seek your higher good in all things.
Stop settling for "good enough."
Raise your level of expectation
Expect great things to happen in your life!

HOPE for the Next Step

November 03

Whenever you experience a "bad day," it is imperative that you look for and affirm a nugget of goodness; it is always there.

Finding the goodness nugget in our most challenging situations may not always be easily recognized, but hindsight proves, it is always there. Trust the Way-maker.

HOPE for the Next Step

November 04

Work on your goals today. Nothing happens, including success, without putting in the work!

Simply wishing your dream would come true will not make it happen. Stay the course and do the work! Every move your make counts.

HOPE for the Next Step

November 05

You are a Star. Every day you are starring in your life's movie. Be sure only what you want on the big screen, appears there.

To become an award-winning version of yourself, set and achieve goals in these seven areas to get started: Professional, Personal, Financial, Mental, Spiritual, Social, and Education. To reach your goals be sure to write them down, develop an action plan, work on the goals daily and assign a time-frame for completion. Otherwise, it is simply a wish.

HOPE for the Next Step

November 06

In a healthy relationship, both parties should embrace, appreciate, and exhibit the same qualities, morals, values, and characteristics you are looking for in the other person.

Know your self-worth. Value each other. Respect is non-negotiable. Happiness, honesty, and trust in a relationship is built and sustained when you both decide to serve each other. That way no one feels neglected and taken for granted.

HOPE for the Next Step

November 07

Father God may Your will be done, and Your words spoken over my life, manifest today. I lay down my will and surrender to Yours, dear Lord.

HOPE for the Next Step

November 08

Your word should be worth its weight in platinum gold. Do not give your word if you do not plan to keep it. Otherwise, it is worthless.

HOPE for the Next Step

November 09

If a thing is not good to do or say on a Sunday, then it is not good to say or do on any day of the week.

Be conscious of the double messages you may be sending to yourself and others.

HOPE for the Next Step

November 10

Speak to me, Lord. I want to hear from you today. I need your wisdom and guidance. My desire is to be obedient to your will. Direct my path so that I will not falter or be confused as to what you want me to do or say.

May the way I live my life inspire others to desire to know more about you. May they know that you always keep your promises.

HOPE for the Next Step

November 11

Today, I will not give in to negative thoughts, negative words or negative people in my life.

These things will no longer hinder me from having a great day and an awesome life.

HOPE for the Next Step

November 12

One of the great benefits of prayer is that you can pray anywhere. You can pray silently in your heart, you can whisper a prayer, or you can pray out loud.

It doesn't matter whether you are kneeling on the floor, lying in bed, standing, at work, in the car, or on a plane. The Father hears us 24 hours a day 7 days a week no matter where we are. This is one of the many benefits He offers us.

HOPE for the Next Step

November 13

I am blessed that I can dream and know that with God's blessings, wisdom, faith, hard work, determination, gratitude and persistence my dreams can become a reality.

HOPE for the Next Step

November 14

Remind someone today that they are not too old to dream. Remind another person that they are not too young to dream.

Dreams come true for those who believe and seek ways to make them happen.

Dreamers recognize, appreciate, and celebrate other dreamers.

HOPE for the Next Step

November 15

It saddens me to know that some people allow others to tell them what they can and cannot become and have in life. Take your power back. Only you can make that decision.

God says you are wonderfully made. He knows this because He, and no one else, made you. He knows exactly what you were created to be. Trust Him.

HOPE for the Next Step

November 16

The science to becoming the person you were meant to be, and having the very best life you can, starts simply with believing you can.

HOPE for the Next Step

November 17

Saying yes to the vision that God gives you opens the door for His supernatural blessings, wisdom, guidance, and provisions to flow freely into your life.

When He beckons to your heart, say "yes," and then be ready to grow closer to Him and receive endless opportunities to enjoy all His promises.

HOPE for the Next Step

November 18

When you give to others freely, it releases the law of reciprocity to act in your favor whenever you need it the most.

Therefore, when you give, you really are receiving at the same time; and you are helping someone in need. It is truly a blessing to be able to give and to receive.

HOPE for the Next Step

November 19

I am thankful for my family and friends who pray for me and encourage me. I am equally thankful that I can pray for and encourage myself as well.

On the days when no one is available to talk with me, or when I feel like being alone, I have learned to remind myself that I am more than a conqueror.

HOPE for the Next Step

November 20

Not only do I know this scripture by memory; I know what it truly means and I live it.

"For I can do everything through Christ, who gives me strength".

Philippians 4:13

HOPE for the Next Step

November 21

I am so amazed that when I changed my old ways of thinking, my life truly changed. I simply started embracing the truth about who I am. This did not happen overnight, and I am still a work in progress. I know without any doubt that we are perfectly and uniquely made.

We are beautiful, intelligent, and we are blessed. All of our steps are divinely ordered. This is our truth!

HOPE for the Next Step

November 22

My sons are an amazing gift to me from God. I am a much better person because they are in my life.

We inspire each other to dream and to never give-up on our dreams.

We love each other through the ups and the downs of life. I am eternally grateful for them. Today, let's praise God for children!

HOPE for the Next Step

November 23

May our family and friends continue to be pure in heart, strong in character, and steadfast in knowing that they matter to all of us.

May we never grow tired of reassuring them of their worth and bright futures.

HOPE for the Next Step

November 24

I've had some days when life was so tough and heavy that I was without the strength or desire to pray.

Yet, the grace of God covered me, gave me hope, and lifted me from my despair. If you ever experience this kind of day, trust God's amazing grace to see you through. He will do the same for you.

HOPE for the Next Step

November 25

Only by God's grace and mercy have we been able to overcome and conquer our fears. His love is everlasting.

Close your eyes, open your heart, and ask Him to bear your burdens.

HOPE for the Next Step

November 26

May we look for the good in everyone we encounter today. Pray for the people you work with. Pray blessings of protection over your family and friends. Pray for the homeless in our city, state, nation, and all over the world.

May the Lord continue to take care of all of their needs, and may we give to them every chance we get without complaining and judging.

HOPE for the Next Step

November 27

Today is going to be an amazing day!

Put on your praise dancing shoes and your shield of faith. Hope for the best in all things for family and friends.

And if negativity tries to steal your joy, you will be happy that you were dressed accordingly!

HOPE for the Next Step

November 28

Lord, may I feel your spirit moving in my soul. May I allow your Spirit to take full control of me.

I surrender my heart's desire to you.

Open my eyes so that I may see the spiritual beauty that you see in me and in others.

HOPE for the Next Step

November 29

Hearing my sons say, "I Love You" when I am having a tough day is music to my ears. However, hearing them remind me that I should pray always soothes my aching heart.

I pray that this book is blessing everyone who is reading it today.

"I love you all and I am always praying for you."

HOPE for the Next Step

November 30

When the trials of life get you down, speak your name out loud to the Father in prayer.

Be sure to do this immediately. Do not allow yourself to lose hope. Be sure to pray for others as they may be going through a tough time, too.

Even when you do not feel like praying, whisper a quick prayer of thanks. This small act of obedience will strengthen you.

HOPE for the Next Step

December 01

"I pray that your hearts will be flooded with light so that you can understand the confident hope he has given to those he called—his holy people who are his rich and glorious inheritance."

Ephesians 1:18

You are a beautiful rose. Yes, a rose has thorns. And yes, you may have some things in your life you want to change.

However, do not let those things define you. You are a rose.

HOPE for the Next Step

December 02

I am thankful for the season I am currently experiencing. Whether I am in a season of prosperity or a season of purging.

For in each season, I am being perfected. I am learning and growing into the person I was created to become.

All precious diamonds are put in the fire to remove imperfections, and I am precious too!

HOPE for the Next Step

December 03

I have learned that everything begets itself and seeks after its own kind. Meaning: whatever you focus on the most will be drawn to you.

In order to get the desired results you desire in life, be intentional on the things and people you concentrate on the most.

For example, if you want happiness do not focus on the people or things that bring you sadness. If you want wealth, do not concentrate on lack or poverty. If you want success, stop focusing on the past mistakes you made.

HOPE for the Next Step

December 04

I have learned through many trials and errors that when I need to write an inspirational poem, a new book, or a thought-provoking response, I must engage my imagination and let it run free.

This is the best way to release and allow creative energy to show us what's really possible for us to achieve. No limits, no excuses, just maximum opportunities.

Release the limits from your imagination and expect to be in awe of the results.

HOPE for the Next Step

December 05

Today, let's choose to live in a managed-stress zone. We pray for and receive God's wisdom, so we can change our limited way of thinking and being.

Doing so helps us to fulfill our destiny.

Affirm out loud "I am free to be healthy, wealthy, and a blessing to others."

HOPE for the Next Step

December 06

As we start making plans to close one year out and live in a new year, let us remember that each day should be lived and not rushed away.

And yes, making plans is a great habit to form. However, never let the busyness of making plans negate the goal of living and appreciating each day.

Let's agree to stop rushing our lives away through unproductive busyness. Let us slow down more to appreciate the gift of life each moment brings.

HOPE for the Next Step

December 07

The number '7' has always been my favorite number. Many years ago, I discovered that the number '7' represents completion. I pray continually that I have the wisdom and strength to complete every endeavor God allows my hands to create.

It is all about starting and completing everything God gives us to do, both the easy things and the things that challenge us. Lord, help us to be finishers!

HOPE for the Next Step

December 08

Today, or tomorrow, is never a good day to give up on your Dream!

Adversity, disappointment, and tears are all a part of the Master Plan. These things are NOT meant to Stop you; the challenges come to help develop your strength and character.

Every beautiful butterfly had to painfully break out of a cocoon. Embrace the process!

HOPE for the Next Step

December 09

I have discovered that waiting on the perfect time to get married, start a family, go back to school, launch a business, lose weight, or start an exercise program is simply an excuse.

Whether motivated by fear, selfishness, or greed, it is still an excuse. Life cannot be put on hold. Furthermore, there is not a "perfect time." The only time we have is now. So today, you might as well pursue the things you have been putting off. You will be amazed at the endless rewards, opportunities, and possibilities made available along the way.

HOPE for the Next Step

December 10

It is reassuring to know that we never walk alone.

We have not cried tears that were not seen nor spoken an unheard prayer, because God is always near. He never rests, slumbers, or sleeps.

No matter the circumstances there is always hope.

HOPE for the Next Step

December 11

Like some of you reading today's inspiration, I have experienced the death of my father and the death of my son. (Just 5 months a part.)

There is no doubt this experience brings with it an unexplainable, devastating, unforgettable, unbearable pain. Yet, with time, if we allow the grace of God, He will cover us like nothing and no one can. He whittles the pain away with each prayer of our own and those made by others on our behalf.

May His peace and love surround you always, especially on the days when there are more questions than answers and more doubt than hope. In Jesus' name, Amen.

HOPE for the Next Step

December 12

I am so glad our job is to love, forgive, and pray for others, not to judge anyone; for I am certain I would not do it with a loving and graceful hand as often as it is required.

Lord, thank you so much for your unconditional love.

May I learn to love others without conditions like Jesus loves me.

HOPE for the Next Step

December 13

God completes and finishes everything He starts.

I pray to be more like my Father in every area of my life.

May I not only start a good work, but may I finish the work He has called and equipped me to do, in excellence.

HOPE for the Next Step

December 14

Our Father wants to bless you. His word says He wants to bless you with the desires of your heart.

Nothing is too small, too big, impossible, or difficult for Him.

Here is our part:
Love. Pray. Ask. Have Faith.
Believe. Have Hope.
Trust. Expect. Be thankful.

HOPE for the Next Step

December 15

Praying is like a two-way radio conversation, not only do you get to speak, you also have to pause to listen while the other person speaks.

Prayer allows us to communicate with our Father anytime and as often as we desire.

During your prayer time, remember to pause after speaking. Give the Father the opportunity to answer.

Also, during the day, and at night, be mindful to be silent and listen for the Father to speak.

HOPE for the Next Step

December 16

As I look back on the times in my life where I was worried, anxious, sad, or lonely, I see the proof of God being there for me. He has never let me down.

Whether I was in need of healing, peace, restoration, renewal, a debt paid, or even a close parking space when it was raining, or I was running late to a meeting; He gives me grace.

His blessings are daily. God's word talks about crooked paths being made straight. He has done this for me many times, even when I questioned His love.

He does this for all His children. He is a good Father.

HOPE for the Next Step

December 17

I walk in favor with God daily. Not because I have been so sweet or righteous. It is not because of anything I have done.

The truth is He does this in spite of the things I have done. He is so special to me because He loved me first. I love Him dearly.

I pray for the unmerited favor of God to reign in your life too.

HOPE for the Next Step

December 18

When everyone appeared to have walked away and turned their back on you and cared less about your pain, God will always allow His "Sonshine" to come through the cloudy days just for you.

That's amazing grace and unconditional love.

HOPE for the Next Step

December 19

Lord, change me. Everyday change me so that I am more like You.

Through my trials and tribulations, Lord, I will keep my faith in you and keep pressing forward; until I see your reflection in me.

Thank you for your everlasting Presence in my life.

HOPE for the Next Step

December 20

Lord, when my days come with a difficult lesson on patience and forgiveness, I trust you.

Lord thank you for the tough lessons learned, for I know it makes me stronger.

Rough times are not made to break us, but to make us better.

HOPE for the Next Step

December 21

Today I am feeling refreshed and exuberant!

Even though sometimes I may feel weary and weak, my faith in You reminds me that I have your wonder-working power within me.

My superpower is my hope in the Lord.

HOPE for the Next Step

December 22

My banker may say no, my doctor may give me a diagnosis I do not want to hear, my friends may walk away.

Yet, the word of God reassures me that His plan is to prosper me and not to harm me.

I believe and have faith that I have everything I need. I am healed, wealthy, and walking in peace.

HOPE for the Next Step

December 23

All the glory and honor belong to the Father.

Every good and perfect gift that we have comes from the Lord. God, you alone are my King.

May the way I live my life speak of your goodness.

HOPE for the Next Step

December 24

To live a life of success, integrity, and prosperity, we must be willing to take the good with the bad.

We love sharing our stories of having wealth, happiness and good times. However, it is usually the stories of our overcoming life's obstacles and adverse circumstances that tend to inspire people to hang in there and to have hope.

HOPE for the Next Step

December 25

In 2 Kings chapter 4, God's words tell of a widow who was down to her last amount of oil.

The prophet tells her to go into the village and collect as many empty jars as she can. She does, and the oil does not run out until the last jar is filled.

This beautiful story of hope reminds us to be a willing vessel, and the Lord will continue to pour into us. Our jars will always overflow.

God always provides the provisions to complete the work He calls us to do. Do not run out of jars. The Lord delights in pouring out blessings to those who are faithful.

HOPE for the Next Step

December 26

A common question people ask is, "What is Faith?" The word tells us in Hebrews 11:1 that faith is the substance of things hoped for, prayed for, and the evidence of things not seen, not yet manifested in the natural.

On a more personal level, this means that for every step ahead of us, and the step we are currently on, He will either carry us over or give us the strength and vision to see more clearly where the next step is located.

Whether it is in darkness or light, we will have everything we need to make the journey one step at a time regardless of how high or wide apart the steps may seem.

HOPE for the Next Step

December 27

If you are having a tough time, and it seems like everyone around you is getting a promotion, a job, married, traveling or starting a successful business, be genuinely happy for them, knowing that there is no such thing as a shortage of good things.

Your time is coming, too. Hang in there. Give yourself the gift of being joyful in all seasons.

HOPE for the Next Step

December 28

Today, do something different. Take a different route to work. Wear your hair in a different style. Pay for someone's lunch. Email a friend just to say, "Hope your day is as wonderful as you are."

Call a distant relative and say, "I just wanted to remind you that I love you."

Buy yourself a bouquet of beautiful flowers at least once a month.

Start celebrating life! It's contagious!

HOPE for the Next Step

December 29

Regardless of how you are feeling right now affirm out loud: "I am Thankful for this beautiful day."

Say out loud, "I have Mountain Moving Faith and Power to make this day awesome."

"I will not accept any negative words spoken over me or over anyone I love. I am triumphant!"

HOPE for the Next Step

December 30

Dreams do come true, as long as you do not water down the original version. Dreams are supposed to be BIG!

Believe in yourself and in your dreams. Regardless of what others have said or may say in the future, they cannot stop you.

You are more powerful than you can imagine. You are unstoppable. You are brilliant, and you are loved. All the great stuff dreams are made of lives in you.

HOPE for the Next Step

December 31

You own the rights to your life. No one else does. Your happiness and success are in your hands.

Therefore, always leave your house in CEO/Boss mode. Look and Act the part. You never know whose path you might cross.

Be Ready. Be Prepared. Be Original. Be Bold. Be Authentic.

When you embrace your brillance, you give others the permission and freedom to embrace theirs.

This is worth celebrating! Throw a party in your honor! You are so amazing! Happy New You!

HOPE for the Next Step

HOPE for the Next Step

TO CONNECT WITH LORETTA McNARY

We would love to read your comments about HOPE for the Next Step. Please email them to:
loretta@lorettamcnary.com

For media inquiries, speaking engagements and public appearances for Loretta McNary, please contact:

Monica Emery of MRE & Associates
909-529-6903 or via email at:
mremediaworks@gmail.com

Website:
www.LorettaMcNary.com

Here are Loretta's social media pages:

Linkedin.com/lorettamcnaryshow
Twitter.com/lorettamcnary
Instagram.com/lorettamcnaryshow
Facebook.com/lorettamcnaryshow
Youtube.com/lorettamcnary
Snapchat.com/lorettamcnary

HOPE for the Next Step

For more inspiration and encouragement, please consider reading Loretta's first book, FAITH for the Next Step. Faith for the Next Step can be ordered on our website or online at Amazon.com.

www.ingramcontent.com/pod-product-compliance
Lightning Source LLC
LaVergne TN
LVHW051541070426
835507LV00021B/2350